# BIG CATS

## Seymour Simon

HarperCollins*Publishers*

The big cats are bundles of muscles ready to spring into action. At rest, they look like giant pussycats, soft and peaceful. But when they are running, climbing, or leaping at their prey, there are few other animals that can match their strength and grace. With claws extended and jaws wide open, the big cats become snarling, slashing hunters. A tiger hits with stunning force and can knock down animals two or three times heavier than itself.

Four kinds of cats can roar: the lion, the tiger, the leopard, and the jaguar. The roaring cats are the group that scientists call "big cats." At one time, scientists thought these cats couldn't also purr. But now scientists have observed purring in all these big cats, particularly in tame, young animals. Three other large cats that cannot roar (but can purr) are the puma, the cheetah, and the snow leopard. In this book, we'll call all seven kinds "big cats."

Some big cats are very big. A large African lion or tiger weighs more than fifty domestic cats and stretches out longer than a horse. The smallest of the big cats in this book weighs about as much as a large dog.

Some kind of big cat is found in every continent of the world except Europe, Australia, and Antarctica. Big cats live in the snowy lands north of the Arctic Circle, in the cool mountains and wide grasslands of temperate climates, and in the steaming rain forests and swamps of the tropics. Though their sizes and the environments in which they live can be very different, the big cats are alike in many ways.

All the members of the cat family (named Felidae) are carnivores—flesh eaters. A big cat, such as this leopard, uses its long, sharp canine teeth to grab and hold down its prey. The side teeth act like knives or shears, slicing up and down to cut through skin and muscle. Even the cat's tongue helps out. The upper surface is covered by tiny rasps or hooks that can scrape the meat from a bone. The largest of the big cats can draw blood just by licking the skin of an animal.

Cats also have razor-sharp claws that are perfect for cutting and holding. The claws are thick and hooked. They can be extended for action, or retracted at will into sheaths in the paws. When the claws are drawn in, cats can run along silently on their soft footpads without alerting their prey.

A cat's senses are very keen, and it can detect its prey at a distance or at night. Sensitive hairs in this jaguar's ears can pick up the sound of an animal's movements even before the animal can be seen. The ears can be turned in different directions so that the jaguar can tell where the sound is coming from.

The long whiskers are special hairs that the cat uses in the dark to feel objects around it. The moist nose is also very sensitive and helps the cat follow its prey's trail by smell.

The eyes of a cat are set far apart and give it a wide field of vision. The big eyes help gather in as much light as possible in the dark. Some light passes through the eyes without being absorbed by light-sensitive cells. Cats have a special lining of reflecting cells at the back of their eyes. The lining acts like a mirror and reflects the light back through the eyes, so that even more light is absorbed. This "mirror" is the reason a cat's eyes seem to shine in the dark.

Cats are mammals. As other mammals do, female big cats give birth to live young. The cubs are born blind and helpless and nuzzle together while the mother is off hunting. Except for the lioness, female big cats raise their cubs alone without any direct help from the male. Most big cats have litters of two or three, but sometimes there are as many as five or six.

This female puma is nursing her two-and-a-half-week-old cubs in a rock den in Montana. At birth a baby puma weighs one pound or less, only a small fraction of the 100 to 200 pounds it will weigh as an adult. By now, the cubs' eyes have opened and their weight has more than doubled.

A female puma nurses her cubs for three or more months, although they begin to eat meat as early as six weeks. In order to feed them, the female is kept busy hunting and killing two or three times as much prey as she needs herself.

Like the other big cats, the puma cubs grow rapidly, doubling their weight almost every week at first. By the age of six months they may weigh thirty to forty pounds. About this time their spots begin to disappear, and in several more months they take on the solid colors of an adult.

The elegantly striped tiger (*Panthera tigris*) is the largest and perhaps the most attractive of all the big cats. It is also the most powerful and dangerous, a solitary hunter with the largest canine teeth of any meat-eating land animal. A large male Siberian tiger may weigh more than 600 pounds and be more than 12 feet long, nose to tail.

There are seven or eight different kinds of tigers left in the world. All of them live in Asia, including the Siberian, Bengal, and Sumatran tigers. Other kinds, such as the Caspian, Chinese, Bali, and Javan tigers may have no more than a few individuals remaining in the wild.

The tiger's coat blends in well with the dark shadows and light patches of the grasslands or forests in which it lives. The stripes hide the tiger and allow it to get close to its prey. Much of a tiger's life is devoted to stalking, killing, and eating food.

The lion (*Panthera leo*) is sometimes called the "King of Beasts." It certainly looks the part: an adult male lion has a noble head and mane, a powerful jaw and sharp teeth, and what seems to be a dignified manner. It can weigh more than 400 pounds and be 9 to 10 feet long. But, of course, there are no "kings" among animals. The lion is no mightier or braver than any of the other big cats. It is a large and strong hunter that kills prey to get its food and survive.

Adding to the lion's "majesty," is its thunderous roar. Both males and females roar. A male lion's roar can be a way of staking out its territory and warning other lions away. Sometimes a lion will stop eating just to let loose with an earsplitting roar. A loud roar can be heard from a distance of five miles. Low roars are used by a female to call her cubs or to locate other lions. Sometimes whole groups of lions, called prides, roar together. Most of the loud group roaring takes place at night, sometimes as a response to the roars of nearby prides or solitary lions.

Most kinds of big cats are solitary—they live and hunt alone most of the time. But lions are different because they are sociable—they live in groups called "prides." A pride includes a number of lionesses and their cubs, along with several males. The members of a pride share an area together and are more or less peaceful among themselves. A pride can have as few as three or four individuals or as many as thirty-five or more. Most prides have at least twice as many females as males.

The lionesses are the core of a pride. They are usually related to each other and remain with the pride all their lives. Males stay with a pride from a few months to several years before they leave by themselves or are driven out by a rival male.

The lionesses share all the chores of the pride. They defend the pride area by driving away any strange females. One or more lionesses guard the cubs while the others are off hunting. The females even suckle each other's cubs, so that a cub may feed from three or four different lionesses to get a full meal. If a lioness dies, her cubs will stay with the pride and be fed by other females. Being a member of a pride is a great advantage for a lion's chance of survival.

While most of the other big cats live in dense forests, swamps, or tropical rain forests, lions usually live in wide-open plains. Only a few hundred years ago, lions roamed wild in parts of Asia and southeastern Europe. But today, their range is much smaller, limited to the central and southern parts of Africa and a small game reserve in India called Gir Forest.

Another advantage of living in a pride is that a group of lions hunting on an open plain is much more successful than a lion hunting alone. Several lions can bring down larger animals and kill more animals on a single hunt. In addition, a pride often eats all of a kill and does not need to guard the remains against hyenas or vultures.

Females usually do most of the hunting. Often, several females will stampede a herd and drive the prey into a trap where other females or males are lying in wait. Once a kill has been made, the stronger males and females eat first, while the cubs and weaker adults scramble for the remains. Sometimes males will share the kill first with cubs rather than with adult females. But when food is scarce, fighting for food can be fierce and some cubs may starve.

The leopard (*Panthera pardus*) is the smallest of the big cats that roar. An adult male leopard usually weighs more than 100 pounds and is about 2 feet high and 7 feet long. It is an excellent climber and very strong for its size. The leopard is also the most graceful and the most successful of the cats at stalking prey. Moving silently and slowly, a leopard can creep up to within a few feet of its prey before it attacks.

Once a leopard catches and kills a large animal such as an impala, it often drags it up a tree to keep it safe from lions, wild dogs, or hyenas. It then feeds on the kill for several days. Leopards rarely kill people, but when they do they can be even more frightening than tigers, because leopards may enter villages during the night and drag the victims from their beds.

The leopard is a very secretive animal and is seldom seen in the wild outside of the protected game preserves of Africa, where it has become accustomed to human visitors. The leopard's secretive nature and the fact that it is at home in a great variety of natural surroundings—from forests and plains to swamps and deserts—make it more likely to survive in modern times than most of the other big cats.

The jaguar (*Panthera onca*) is the largest cat to be found in the Americas. Big males weigh from 200 to 300 pounds and can be as long as 7 feet. Jaguars range from Mexico south through Central and South America. The jaguar is more heavily built and muscled than a leopard and has a wider face, but the two big spotted cats are alike in many other ways—they are strong, adaptable, and secretive.

The jaguar is a good climber, an excellent swimmer, and roams through dense rain forests with ease. It regularly preys on animals two or three times bigger than itself, and can drag its prey for miles to a safe place to eat. While lions, tigers, and leopards usually kill their prey with a bite to the soft throat, jaguars often bite right through the bony skull of an animal. A jaguar can kill a smaller animal just by slapping it on the head with a paw.

Jaguars usually hunt by walking along a river or a trail in the forest until they see prey. The jaguar's main food is the capybara, the largest rodent in the world, with a weight of 100 pounds. But jaguars also prey on a long list of animals including wild pigs, monkeys, deer, caimans, cattle, horses, and dogs.

The spotted leopard and the black leopard, or black panther, are just variations of the same species. The spotted leopard is usually found in the plains or open forests of Africa, where its spotted coat blends in perfectly with the grasses or branches. The black leopard is more often found in the dark rain forests of Asia or Africa. When it is in bright light, you can see the spots in the fur. Despite what some people think, black leopards are no fiercer or stronger than the spotted kind. Jaguars, like leopards, can also be black. But their coats are so dark that they appear jet-black, and the spots are very difficult to see even in bright light.

The largest cat of North America is the puma (*Felis concolor*). The puma goes by many other names, including mountain lion, cougar, panther, painter, silver lion, mountain devil, mountain screamer, and catamount (cat of the mountain). Whatever it is called, the puma was an important part of the folklore of many native American peoples and early settlers in the West. Some native Americans so respected the puma that they refused to kill it or protect their livestock from its attack.

Only a bit smaller than the jaguar, the puma weighs up to 200 pounds. Its color varies from tan to dark brown, with white underparts. The puma is a marvelous hunter. It has sharp claws and long canine teeth, and great strength and speed. It can bring down animals as large as bighorn sheep or elk, and can catch animals as small and quick as this snowshoe hare.

The puma is also an amazing leaper. Its long, thick tail helps balance the puma during a jump. One report credits a puma with vaulting a nine-foot fence while holding a sheep in its mouth.

The puma ranges from Alaska and Canada deep into South America, and from a few feet above sea level to the tops of high mountains. In the United States, most pumas are found west of the Mississippi River, except for a small population in Florida.

The cheetah (*Acinonyx jubatus*) is the fastest land animal in the world over short distances. It usually hunts in the wide-open plains or open woodlands of Africa. Instead of stalking its prey, a cheetah may walk or bound toward a herd of gazelles until they start to run. The cheetah chooses one animal and pursues only that one until it is caught, or the cheetah gives up.

In a few seconds, a cheetah can go from zero to seventy miles per hour. That's faster than the fastest racehorse. The cheetah's body coils and uncoils like a steel spring. Often, all four of its feet are off the ground at the same time. It almost seems to be flying.

Once the cheetah is within striking distance, it slows down to follow each turn of its prey. The cheetah can turn its body in midair so that it can chase closely after its zigzagging target. Yet, if the gazelle could hold out for just a few minutes, it would be safe, because the cheetah can only maintain its speed for a few hundred yards.

After the kill, the prey is eaten quickly on the spot or dragged to cover. Cheetahs can't defend their kill against packs of hyenas, lions, leopards, or even a large gathering of vultures. Both lions and leopards will attack and kill cheetahs if they can. If the cheetah does get a chance to finish its meal, it leaves and makes no attempt to come back for seconds.

The cheetah looks different from the other big cats. It has a small head with no large canine teeth, a lean body with a broad chest, a long tail for balance, and long slender legs with blunted unsheathed claws like those of a dog. An adult male weighs about 130 pounds and reaches a length of nearly 7 feet. Cheetahs are found in Africa south of the Sahara Desert, and in very small numbers on the Arabian Peninsula.

Three to six cheetah cubs are born in a litter. The young cubs are silver gray or white on top, with dark, spotted undersides. When they are very young, the cubs remain hidden when their mother goes off to hunt. After three months, they begin to follow their mother and wait on the sidelines while she hunts. The mother uses a kind of chirping to call her cubs to feed on the kill. When the cubs rest next to their mother, the whole group purrs loudly.

Cheetahs are one of the most endangered big cats. Even though they produce cubs frequently, many of the cubs die because the female is unable to defend them against predators such as a lion, leopard, or a pack of hyenas. Also, the herds of animals upon which the cheetah preys are disappearing as human pressure increases to use the land for farming.

The rarest of the big cats is the snow leopard (*Uncia uncia*). It lives in the high, jagged mountains of the Himalayas and Central Asia. Long, thick fur insulates the snow leopard against freezing temperatures and howling winds. Slightly smaller than the spotted leopard, the snow leopard weighs about 100 pounds, with a head and body length of 3 to 4 feet.

The snow leopard has thick paws, with the front ones much larger than the hind ones. Its bushy tail is almost as long as its body. The large paws and tail help balance the leopard on the steep slopes of the snow-covered mountains. The cat is a mighty leaper, able to jump forty-five feet across a snowy gorge or spring onto a high rocky ledge without climbing. It preys upon mountain goats, sheep, and smaller animals such as rodents.

The snow leopard's handsome fur has caused it to be much in demand. Despite a ban on hunting in many countries, and a worldwide campaign by conservationists to save the snow leopard, an illegal trade in the animal's pelt still continues. Fewer than a thousand of these cats may be left in the wild. The future of the beautiful snow leopard remains very much in doubt.

Almost all the wild cats, big and small, have been relentlessly hunted and trapped by people. Throughout history, thousands upon thousands of tigers and lions have been hunted down in the name of sport. In the 1960's and 1970's, the demand for fur coats made from the skins of spotted cats led to widespread killing of the leopard, cheetah, and jaguar, along with smaller spotted cats such as the snow leopard and clouded leopard. The puma has also been trapped and poisoned for being a killer of livestock.

Though some of the big cats are now protected by laws in many countries, illegal killing still goes on. Of even more concern is that as more and more land is taken from the wild, there is less and less room for the big cats to live.

What can we do to save the big cats? We can support laws to stop the sale and use of wild cat skins around the world. We can help wildlife organizations and encourage governments to set up preserves where big cats will be safe. We can learn to treasure the wildlife on our planet instead of destroying it. The future of the big cats is up to us.

Library of Congress Cataloging-in-Publication Data
Simon, Seymour.
    Big cats / Seymour Simon.
        p.      cm.
    Summary: Describes the physical characteristics, habits, and natural
environment of various species of big cats.
    ISBN 0-06-021646-8. — ISBN 0-06-021647-6 (lib. bdg.)
    1. Felidae—Juvenile literature.      [1. Felidae.    2. Cats.]    I. Title.
QL737.C23S56   1991                                                    90-36374
599.74'428—dc20                                                        CIP
                                                                        AC

Photo credits:
Jacket and pp. 9, 37 © Lynn M. Stone; pp. 1, 2-3, 5, 11, 15, 16, 23, 24,
27, 31, 32, 39 © Jeanne Drake; pp. 7, 34 © Joe McDonald; pp. 12, 28,
40 © Alan & Sandy Carey; pp. 18, 20 © David Reuther.